TIME MANAGEMENT

BULLET GUIDE

Mac Bride

About the author

Mac Bride saw his first book published in 1982, and since then he has written something over 120 books on various aspects of programming, computer applications, the Internet, language for house buyers, green issues and other topics. As well as writing, he has edited and typeset books on subjects ranging from marketing through feng shui to postmodernism. Balancing the needs of the job against the demands of being an active father, grandfather, DIY-er and chair of governors, he has learnt a lot about time management – and never fails to find time to relax in the kitchen, or the cinema, or playing with his grandchildren.

TIME
MANAGEMENT

BULLET GUIDE

Hodder Education, 338 Euston Road, London NW1 3BH

Hodder Education is an Hachette UK company.

First published in UK 2011 by Hodder Education.

This edition published 2011.

Copyright © 2011 Mac Bride

The moral rights of the author have been asserted.

Database right Hodder Education (makers)

Artworks (internal and cover): Peter Lubach
Cover concept design: Two Associates

British Library Cataloguing in Publication Data: a catalogue record for this title is available from the British Library.

10 9 8 7 6 5 4 3 2 1

The publisher has used its best endeavours to ensure that any website addresses referred to in this book are correct and active at the time of going to press. However, the publisher and the author have no responsibility for the websites and can make no guarantee that a site will remain live or that the content will remain relevant, decent or appropriate.

The publisher has made every effort to mark as such all words which it believes to be trademarks. The publisher should also like to make it clear that the presence of a word in the book, whether marked or unmarked, in no way affects its legal status as a trademark.

Every reasonable effort has been made by the publisher to trace the copyright holders of material in this book. Any errors or omissions should be notified in writing to the publisher, who will endeavour to rectify the situation for any reprints and future editions.

Hachette UK's policy is to use papers that are natural, renewable and recyclable products and made from wood grown in sustainable forests. The logging and manufacturing processes are expected to conform to the environmental regulations of the country of origin.

www.hoddereducation.co.uk

Typeset by Stephen Rowling/Springworks.

Printed in Spain.

Contents

Introduction

The basic laws of physics tell you that time is finite and that its progress cannot be stopped or slowed. You cannot manage time. However, you can manage your use of time, and that's what this little book is all about. ('Manage how you use your time' wouldn't fit on the cover, so we went for the shorter – if inaccurate – 'Time management'.)

There are four main strands to better use of time:

* setting priorities, then allocating time by those priorities
* organizing your schedule and your working space
* limiting other people's demands on your time
* knowing when to stop work on a job.

I hope that the time you invest in working through this book will yield big dividends in reducing the pressures on your time. And, in the interests of not wasting any more of your time, I'll stop right there and let you get on with it.

1 Be a Time Lord (or Lady)

You're feeling the pressure. There aren't enough hours in the day to fit in all the things you need to do. What's the answer?

Well, you can't make more time – we all have 24 hours in each day – so you have to:

* spend less time doing some things, and/or
* stop doing some things altogether.

Which raises the questions:

* Which things?
* How do I cut down the time I spend on them?

You can't make more time – we all have 24 hours in each day

The aim of this book is to help you to find more time to do the things you want to – whether that is work, family, friends or fun related.

● Find more time for the things you want to do

Saving time takes time

Improving your time management means changing your habits, and that takes effort. But, more to the point, analysing the way you currently spend your time, and working out what you could change and how to change it, all takes time – which you are short of!

The initial investment of time can be very small, and can be done while you are doing something else. You need to think, and you can do that while on the bus or in the bath. Identify one thing that you could spend less time on – or stop doing – for the next couple of weeks. Use that time to read this book, then start working through the five-step time saver.

4

The five-step time saver

1 Use the time you have freed up to do a simple analysis of the ways you spend your time.

2 From that analysis, identify a few things that you could do less or not at all.

3 Reinvest some of the extra free time to do a more thorough analysis of your habits.

4 Identify and implement other time savers.

5 Make good use of your new free time.

The key is not in spending time, but in investing it.

Stephen R. Covey

The first cut

The simplest way to reduce the pressure on your time is to stop doing something. Cutting out the second coffee of the morning, and the gossip at the coffee machine, could free up 20 minutes of work time. Giving up *EastEnders* will release you for 2 hours a week to do other things.

But perhaps there's nothing you want to stop doing, and it may not – in the long run – be necessary.

If the reason you are short of time is poor organization and inefficient habits, reorganizing the way you do things could solve the problem. But it takes time to reorganize, so you need to create some slack, somehow, now.

6

But there's nothing I can give up!

Not even for a few weeks? If that really is the case, then can you find some reading, thinking and planning time elsewhere?

- on the train/tube/bus while commuting to and from work
- while having your lunchtime sandwich
- while waiting for your supper to cook
- during the last 15 minutes or so of the evening, instead of lying in bed worrying about all the stuff you've got to get through tomorrow.

Until we can manage time, we can manage nothing else.

Peter F. Drucker

Know your enemy

Time is not the enemy. The enemy is – and I hate to say this – you, or rather the way you allocate your time. The good news is that you can change it.

First, you have to analyse what you are doing. Keep a diary for the next week – working days and weekend. This needs to be detailed, because the devil is in the detail. There's an example opposite. This is just for the morning at work – your diary should run from getting up to going back to bed at the end of the day.

Time is not the enemy. The enemy is you

Will this diarist ever get that report finished? Two things leap out from this diary:

✱ Three coffee breaks is at least one too many.
✱ You don't need to check your email every hour.

There's more to see here. Let's look at the patterns of time (next page).

9.05	Arrive at work
9.10	Make coffee, chat
9.20	Check email, follow up web link from Cathy
9.35	Work on report
9.55	Find figures for Mike
10.15	Check email
10.20	Work on report
10.35	Make coffee, catch up with Jerry from marketing
10.55	Work on report
11.05	Phone call from boss, asking about the report
11.15	Work on report
11.25	Check email
11.35	Work on report
11.55	Make coffee, chat
12.05 – 12.35	Work on report

The patterns of time

This exercise works best in colour (publisher, please note), and using graph paper will produce a neater result. You turn the diary data into a timeline, with each type of activity displayed as a block of a different colour. There are two ways to do this:

＊ Put each activity on a separate line. This shows the frequency and spacing of activities – look how the coffee and email break up the morning. It can also show why things take so long to do. Look how the main task has been broken into seven chunks, some as short as ten minutes. Stopping and starting breaks the flow and costs time.

＊ Combine them on a single line. The advantage of this is that you can fit a whole working week on a single page, and then compare one day with another, looking for regular patterns.

10

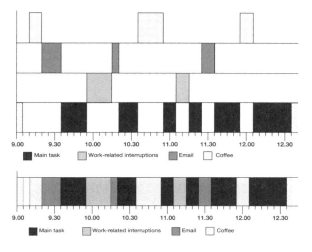

Activity timelines – you really need bright colours to make the single lines readable.

2 Priorities and targets

It can take a little time and effort to sort out your priorities and targets for daily life, and even more so for the longer term, but it is an essential early step towards taking control of your time.

* You need to be clear about what your priorities are – as distinct from those of people around you.
* You need to know which things are most important, so that, if you run short of time, it's the less important stuff that gets left undone.

Rule number 1: Your priorities must have top priority

. . . .

In the long run, men only hit what they aim at.
Henry David Thoreau

● Don't be afraid to aim high

Your targets ...

Take a little time out of your busy life to think about the following
questions on two timescales – the 10- to 30-year long-term and the
one- to five-year short term:

✳ What do you want out of your life?
✳ Is that different from what you have now?
✳ How can you best achieve the changes or maintain what you have?
✳ Which aspects of your future life are most important to you?

And remember, you do not have to be driven or achieve great heights.
Being happy and comfortable is a valid life aim.

My life has no purpose, no direction, no aim, no meaning, and yet I'm happy. I can't figure it out. What am I doing right?

Snoopy

... and priorities

Your targets are the things you aim to do or be; your priorities set the order in which you do things and the amount of effort you put into them. They should arise from your targets. Take each of your targets in turn and ask these questions:

* What do I need to do to achieve this?
* What do I need to do first, then next?
* Will what I am doing now help me to achieve this target?

There's more on targets and planning in the next chapter.

You've got to think about 'big things' while you're doing small things, so that all the small things go in the right direction.

Alvin Toffler

Whose priorities?

How far are your priorities your own? We all play multiple roles as workers, parents, partners, children, friends and members of other groups. All of these impose some priorities on us, and we must accept at least some of these to fulfil the roles properly. If you feel that other people's priorities are pushing into the queue ahead of yours, that can be a source of stress.

This may be most obvious at work. Tasks should be prioritized in this order:

1 the requirements of your defined job
2 the demands of those higher up the line
3 the requests of colleagues.

But within that are different levels of priority.

Combining priorities

Don't let other people's high priorities push yours aside. Keep the job manageable by dealing with your own priorities first.

See 'How to say "no" at work' and 'How to say "no" to the boss' in Chapter 7.

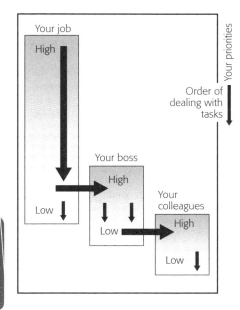

Urgent and important

There's a big difference between urgent and important:

* Urgent means it has to be done quickly.
* Important means it has to be done well.

When setting priorities remember:

* Some urgent things are not important.
* Some important things are not urgent.
* What is important and/or urgent to someone else may be neither to you.

When jobs are piling up, assess their urgency and importance, then tackle them in the order opposite (follow the numbers!). Allocate time for important jobs when they arrive, even if you keep them until later.

There's a big difference between urgent and important

Urgency

3 Do this next

1 Do this now!

Importance

5 Does this need doing at all?

2 Schedule time for this

4 Do it

The work–life balance

There is no ideal, quantifiable work–life balance – 50:50 or 80:20, or whatever. We each need to find our own balance, based partly on our targets and partly on the other people in our life, because they are part of the balance. You will find it useful to ask for their opinions when answering these questions:

- How often does your work interfere with your social/family/love life? Never, sometimes, regularly?
- How often does your outside life interfere with your job? Never, sometimes, regularly?

In both cases 'interfere with' may mean 'prevent you from being there when you are supposed to be' or 'occupy your thoughts so that you cannot participate properly'.

Finding the balance

If other people's answer to either question is 'regularly' – even though you would say 'sometimes' – you need to find a better balance, because the current one is causing you stress.

1 Think again about your targets. Are they mutually compatible? Which is most important?
2 Compare your priorities for each target, looking for clashes. Are your career priorities clashing with those of your social/love life? Even if there is no actual clash, which should take precedence?
3 Try to identify two or three achievable changes to your routine that would help to improve the balance.

3 Organize your time

Organized people get more stuff done because they:

* know what the next job is so can get on with it as soon as the last one is done
* have allocated sufficient time to the job
* have the paperwork/files/materials they need to hand.

Organized people organize both their **time** and their **space**.

> I am definitely going to take a course on time management ... just as soon as I can work it into my schedule.
> Louis E. Boone

Organized people get more stuff done

Targets and timetables

There is more to organizing your time than writing activities into your diary – although that is essential. You need to start from your targets.

1 Take each long-term target in turn, starting with the most important.
2 Work out where you want to be on the path towards it by the end of the year.
3 Work out what you need to do each month to achieve that goal.
4 Allocate time in your diary for doing those things …
5 … then do them.

Get smart!
When setting yourself tasks, use the SMART approach. See next page.

SMART planning

Your long-term targets may be quite vague – becoming a senior executive, getting rich, raising a family – but you should be able to identify specific goals along the way. It is the actions needed to reach these goals that need to be written into your forward planning.

For example, you want to be a senior executive in an international company and know that it would help if you spoke French so that you could socialize with people in the Paris office. Learning conversational French is then your goal for the year, and mastering one hour of the Michel Thomas course could be the goal each month. These are SMART goals.

SMART goals

Specific – clearly defined. 'Get fitter' is not specific. 'Run a mile in under six minutes' is.

Measurable – how will you know when you have reached it? Will you have a certificate, a new skill, a physical object, a chunk of money in the bank?

Achievable – is it within your capabilities, and do you have the time and other resources that you need?

Rewarding – in what way will you be better off for doing it?

Time-based – when must it be done by?

Diaries, calendars and organizers

Whether you use an electronic or a paper diary, calendar or organizer is largely irrelevant – use whatever you prefer or your organization dictates. What's important is how you use it.

The key thing is to have only one in which you record your meetings and activities. It may be a smallish (page-a-day) paper diary, a personal digital assistant (PDA) or a smartphone, but must be something that can be kept with you at all times so that appointments can be recorded as soon as they are made.

Holidays, meetings and other times when you are definitely not available can then be copied on to a public wall calendar, or shared electronic calendar.

30

Diary/PDA/smartphone

For your eyes only.

Only you can write in it.

Records all activities.

With you at all times.

Updated immediately with
changes.

Detailed breakdown of your
work time.

Public calendar

Visible to colleagues/friends.

Certain people may be able to
book time.

Shows only what's relevant to
other people.

Fixed location.

Synchronized with your diary
regularly.

Shows work time blocked out.

Filling the diary

Your diary is not just for recording appointments. It is your key tool for ensuring that you have time to do the things you need and want to do. Use it to allocate time for routine chores at work (and in your personal life) and for specific tasks and projects. These can range from a 15 minute planning slot every Monday to the greater part of every available day over a long period to deal with a major project. The point is, if you allocate time to everything you do, you can see what time is available – if any – for other things.

Allocate time according to your priorities and in a way that gets jobs done with minimal stress.

Your diary is your key tool for ensuring that you have time for the things you want to do

Allocating time by priorities

Fill your diary in this order:

1 any commitments carried over from the old diary
2 family holidays, medical appointments and other personal activities (when you start the diary, or as soon as you know about them)
3 time for SMART activities leading to your long-term targets (at the start of the year or every month)
4 meetings and other work activities involving other people (as they are planned)
5 if appropriate, time for specific projects (working back from the due date).

When you check your diary each morning, check that there is at least half an hour's free time in there, to be ready for the unexpected.

See Chapter 5 for more on allocating time to jobs.

Blocks of time

Stopping and starting wastes time. This is true for every type of job. Each time you restart, you have to get your equipment and materials together, look back over what you have done and think through where to go next. Some stops are a good thing – you need regular breaks on big jobs – some are unavoidable, but others are under your control.

When allocating time in your diary, write in either a solid block big enough to get the whole job done, or a set of blocks, each of a good working length.

See Chapter 8 for guidelines on limiting interruptions.

Mind the gaps

Even with the best organized diary you will still get gaps – mostly waiting
for things. Each gap may only be a few moments, but they can build
up over the day. This is time spent waiting for the computer to start up,
documents to download or print, people to arrive for meetings. Does
it have to be wasted time, or can you make good use of it? Depending
upon how much time you have, and whether you are in the office or
not, you could:

✳ Filter your paperwork (see Chapter 4).

✳ Do some filing (see Chapters 4 and 10).

✳ Reinvigorate yourself with a quick relax (see the *Beat Stress* bullet guide).

✳ Think through a forthcoming job.

4 Organizing your workspace

In a well-organized workspace, you don't waste time looking for stuff. The aim is a zero clutter workspace where:

* What you need is either immediately to hand or in its proper place.
* What you don't need right now is stored where it can be found.
* What you don't need ever again is thrown away.

Be ruthless. If you don't need to keep it for your records, or for reuse, or for the taxman, or in case of disputes, out it goes.

A well organized workspace has zero clutter

● Your key tool for organizing paper. If you don't need it, bin it!

Two other useful tools for organizing your paperwork are a filing cabinet for long-term storage, and a large bulldog clip for keeping together those things that need to be dealt with as soon as possible.

Taming the paperwork

Clear your desk by following this process. It can be done in stages if there's too much for one session.

Gather the papers into one big pile. The aim is to reduce it as painlessly as possible. First, sort it quickly into four piles. If you can't decide immediately what to do with something, put it in pile 4.

1 stuff to throw away – straight in the bin
2 things to be filed
3 things to be dealt with
4 things that you don't know what to do with.

The man whose life is devoted to paperwork has lost the initiative. He is dealing with things that are brought to his notice, having ceased to notice anything for himself.

C. Northcote Parkinson

The next stage is to do your filing, then start working through your 'to be dealt with' pile. You can probably use gaps to do some of this (see 'Mind the gaps' in Chapter 3).

Your paper mountain is now a molehill. Go back to your 'don't know' pile and sort it, taking more time to think about things. You might like to get some advice on what's left in the 'don't know' pile this time.

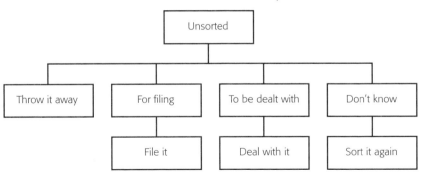

Keeping control

Once you've cleared that paperwork mountain, you do not want to let it grow again. Apply these rules to all new paperwork as it arrives.

1 If you do not need it, throw it away.
2 If you can deal with it right now, do so, then file it or throw it away.
3 If you don't have the time to deal with it now, put it in a pile, held by a clip, to deal with later.

You should only ever have one pile of paper – and even this should never have more than a few items in it. Allocate time in your diary, and aim to clear it each day.

Once you've cleared that paperwork mountain, don't let it grow again

● The paperless office is a myth, but the less-paper office is real and can be achieved

The electronic workspace

You should take the same zero-clutter approach to your electronic
workspace for the same reasons. Unused programs and unwanted files
waste time – they slow down you and your computer.

Clear the desktop!

Start by clearing the desktop. The only things you should have on here
are shortcuts to programs or folders that you use pretty much every day.

1 Delete any shortcuts that you do not regularly use – you can
  recognize a shortcut by the arrow.
2 Create a folder (right-click on the desktop, point to New and then
  click on Folder). Call it 'Clutter'.
3 Move everything, apart from the useful shortcuts, into the Clutter
  folder. We'll deal with it later.

Prune your programs

The only programs that you should keep are those that you use and those that the computer needs to function. If you have any that have not been used in the last year, remove them – if they are set to check for updates automatically, they may be slowing your computer down, whether you use them or not.

1 Open the Control Panel.
2 Select Uninstall a program (Vista or Windows 7) or Add/Remove Programs (XP).
3 If you use a program, leave it.
4 If you don't know what a program does, leave it – it may be needed by the system or your web browser.
5 If you know you don't use it or need it, uninstall it.

Filing for speed

The rules here are:

* Don't keep it if you don't need it.
* Otherwise put it where you can find it again easily.

There should be only one

While you are working on a project, you might have several versions of it as you try out different approaches. Once it is finalized, you should delete the unused versions and any other files accumulated along the way but not needed in the end – unless you have very specific reasons for keeping them. If you need to go back to the project later, you shouldn't have to waste time sorting through multiple versions.

46

Folders: smaller is better

You can normally store documents wherever you like on a PC. They can all go into *My Documents*, but the more files you have in a folder, the longer it takes to find the one you want.

Aim for a maximum of 20–30 files, and no more than 20 sub-folders within any folder. What works best varies, but you should have a folder for each set of documents – e.g. those for a client or a project. If there are lots of files, then subdivide the folder by time or some aspect of the work.

If you have lots of folders, group them into higher level folders. It is simpler to click down through three levels of folders than to hunt through a list of 100 files.

5 Big jobs and little jobs

Some jobs are of known duration – a three-hour training session, a one-day visit to a distant client. Others are task based – researching and writing a report, decorating a birthday cake, carving a replacement table leg. Before you commit to the job, you need to assess how long it will take and check that it can be fitted into your schedule.

Always allow yourself enough time!

The five minute do-it-yourself job

Anyone who has done any kind of DIY – mending a fuse, hanging a picture, fixing a dripping tap, or whatever – will recognize this.

A five minute DIY job can only be done in five minutes if:

* You have all the tools and materials at hand at the start.
* You really do know what you are doing
* Nothing goes wrong.
* Nothing interrupts you.
* The gods smile on you.

Assessing the job

The need to allocate enough time to jobs is just as true for little jobs as it is for big ones. Even a little job over-running will put your schedule under pressure, and that puts you under stress.

This is also just as true for household chores as it is for projects at work. Value your time – and yourself – properly.

How much time do you need to do this job?

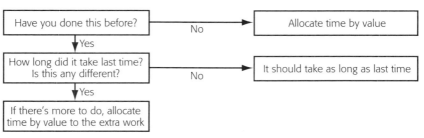

Have you done this before? ── No ──▶ Allocate time by value

▼ Yes

How long did it take last time? Is this any different? ── No ──▶ It should take as long as last time

▼ Yes

If there's more to do, allocate time by value to the extra work

When you've got a realistic estimate of the time, add on extra for things going wrong. As a rough guide, add 10% for simple jobs, and a further 10% for every extra complexity or other person involved. At worst, you should still finish within the available time; at best, you will have spare time to relax or get on with something else.

Now get out your diary and write in the time you need to do the job. This may be a single continuous block, or spread out over a period.

Even the little job, if it over-runs, will put you under stress

Allocating time by value

There are some things that you have to do just because you have to do them, particularly if you are in any kind of public sector work. But, generally, you should be able to allocate a value to the task – either money saved or money earned. From that figure you can calculate how much time to allow for it:

1 Write down the value of the task.
2 Subtract the cost of any materials needed.
3 Divide by your hourly (or daily) rate.

The result is the number of hours (days) that can be spent on it.

If you have the time, and are confident it will be enough, take the job on.

✳ If the time is not available, don't do it.
✳ If the time is clearly not going to be long enough, don't do it.

Nosnikrap's Wal

Parkinson's Law states:
'Work expands so as to fill the time available for its completion.'

Nosnikrap's Wal states:
'Work contracts to fit into the available time.'

And this is often true, especially with open-ended jobs. If you are asked to write a summary report on something that you know quite well – so you don't have to research it first – you could probably do just as good a job in two hours as in a whole day.

Doing things by halves

You have a deadline. Here's a simple technique to help ensure that the job is done on time.

1 Before you start, decide on the half-way marker for the job.
2 When you are half-way through the available time, check the job.
3 If you are less than half-way through it, take a few moments to reassess the job. What can be simplified? What can be omitted? Can anyone else do part of it?
4 Set a new schedule, allowing the time to extend into some – not all – of the extra time.
5 Set a new marker for where you should be half-way through the remaining time.
6 Repeat steps 2 and 3.

With more complex jobs and longer deadlines, you should set progress targets at regular intervals from early on to keep the job on track.

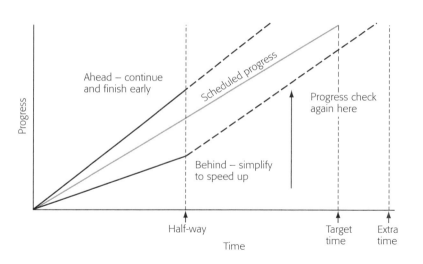

Ahead – continue and finish early

Scheduled progress

Progress check again here

Behind – simplify to speed up

Progress

Half-way

Target time

Extra time

Time

Working smarter not harder

Before you start any job, ask yourself these questions:

1 Does this really need doing?

If 'yes', then:

2 Am I the best person to do it? (Does it need more/fewer skills? Is there anyone else?)

If 'yes', then spend time preparing before you do anything.

* Look back at similar jobs you've done in the past. What can you learn from those?
* Think the job through in outline and decide the best way to tackle it.
* Now think through the details and see what you've missed.
* Work out what resources it will need, and make sure that they are available.
* Decide how you will tell when the job is done.

58

When is the job done?

If you work for someone else, and a job is finished when the boss says so, stop reading now.

With some jobs, the answer is simple: the car is repaired when it's working again; the database is up to date when all current data have been entered into it. Others may be harder to sign off. At what point do you stop rewriting a report?

Nothing is ever perfect. If the job is done well enough to meet or exceed the boss's/client's/public's expectations, that is good enough.

Give me six hours to chop down a tree, and I will spend the first four hours sharpening the axe.

Abraham Lincoln

6 Working with others

Time spent with others is generally time well spent. Co-operation can reduce the time a job takes and make it easier and more fun. However, some people waste your time:

1 **The underemployed** – managers who fill their days with meetings, and colleagues who don't have enough to do.
2 **The disorganized** – who will send you on wild goose chases, and leave messes for you to clear up.
3 **The overworked** – who will try to off-load some of their excess on to you.

Other people can save you time or waste it

● The weekly meeting: waiting for the boss who will tell them, as usual, about the need for greater efficiency

Time spent supporting people – through a difficulty at work or a personal crisis – may disrupt your own schedule, but it's not a waste of time if it helps them to cope.

Meetings: (1) Why meet?

Meetings enable groups to work better. They may be held to:

* update people on progress
* share information and ideas
* decide what to do next
* allocate tasks and responsibilities
* reinforce group identity.

If the only purpose is to reinforce group identity, then a social activity is probably more effective than a meeting.
If information is being given out, without discussion, meetings are rarely the most efficient way to do this.

Meetings are indispensable when you don't want to do anything.

J.K. Galbraith

The following are not valid reasons for holding a meeting:

✳ We always have one on Tuesdays.
✳ People like us are supposed to have meetings.
✳ We need to arrange a meeting.

You should only be at a meeting if:

✳ you have something to contribute, and/or
✳ you will gain something from it.

If all you are doing is observing, you shouldn't be there. Keep abreast of what's going on by reading the minutes.

Meetings: (2) Making best use

Make the best use of meetings, and encourage the other participants to
do the same.

Be prepared

1 If you are in charge of the meeting, create an agenda and get it out to
   the participants in good time.
2 Don't put 'any other business' on the agenda. If people want to raise
   matters, they should let you know in advance.
3 If there are documents to be discussed, circulate them beforehand.
4 Read the agenda, the minutes of the last meeting and any
   documents before you go.
5 Make note of any points you want to raise.
6 Be there on time. And, if you are in charge, start on time.

66

Stick to the agenda

If you are running the meeting:

* Agree an end time before you start, and keep to it.
* If it's a full agenda, set time limits for items.
* Keep the meeting to the agenda.
* Encourage participation, but …
* … make sure that people stick to the point.

And, if you are not running the meeting, try to encourage whoever is to follow these rules.

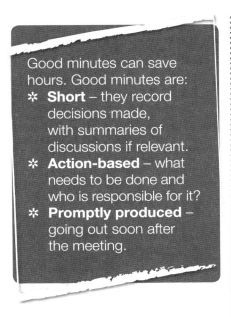

Good minutes can save hours. Good minutes are:

* **Short** – they record decisions made, with summaries of discussions if relevant.
* **Action-based** – what needs to be done and who is responsible for it?
* **Promptly produced** – going out soon after the meeting.

67

The art of delegation

Properly done, delegation can be a great time saver (at least, it will save your time). For success, the person you are delegating to must have:

* the ability to do the job
* the skills that the job needs
* a clear understanding of what is required.

If any one of these is missing, you may well spend longer sorting out the mess than you would have spent doing the job yourself. It's up to you to ensure that the skills and understanding are in place.

68

Properly done, delegation can be a great time saver

Training for delegating

Training is an investment. It takes time, but it should save you more in the long run. There are broadly three stages:.

1 Hand holding

You are with the trainee all the way through.

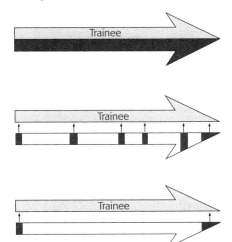

2 Checkpoints

Progress is checked and corrected at key points – requires small inputs of time, though they can interrupt other workflow.

3 Full delegation

You hand the job over at the start, and collect it at the end. Major time saving!

Time wasters

Some people are real time wasters, and most of us are, to a lesser extent, on occasion. How do we waste other people's time? And how can we best handle time wasters?

Time waster: 'Thought I'd ring for a chat.' [Bored at work]

Avoiding action: 'How nice! But can I ring you back later? I'm due in a meeting.'

TW: Making any other phone call when you need to work uninterrupted

AA: Don't answer (see Chapter 8)

TW: 'Would you do this little thing for me?'

AA: 'No.' [But nicely, see Chapter 7]

TW: 'You must have a look at this website!'

AA: 'Thanks. I'll do that later.'

TW: 'Do you fancy a quick coffee/drink/lunch?'

AA: 'No.' [But nicely, see Chapter 7 – unless you are thirsty/hungry or want to socialize with or talk to TW privately]

Don't waste their time
Do as you would be done by! If you catch yourself wasting other people's time, stop.

7 The art of saying 'no'

Saying 'no' can be a great time saver. It can free up the time that would be spent doing things that matter to other people, and leave more time to do things that matter to you.

If you are the sort of polite, obliging person who likes to get on with other people, then saying 'no' can be a little stressful – but it doesn't have to be, and it gets much easier with practice.

We all have limits to what we can do well, and other people may need to be told this

Do you need to learn how to say 'no'?

It's nice to be popular, and flattering that people see you as the one who can get things done, but sometimes it can become too much. You need to learn how to say 'no' if:

1 At work, you are struggling to find time to complete your own jobs.
2 At work or at home, you feel that you are doing more than your fair share.
3 In your social life, you agree to do things that you don't really want to do.

The bad news is time flies.
The good news is you're the pilot.

Michael Altshuler

How to say 'no' at work

The next time someone asks you to do something for which you don't have time, say 'No'. Follow these guidelines, and you can say 'no' without getting stressed or creating a difficult situation:

✳ Refuse the request, not the person. You are willing to help, but don't have the time.
✳ Refuse with a smile. There's no point in making enemies, and you may want help another day.
✳ Make it clear that you have your own priorities. Your own work must come first.
✳ Make helpful suggestions, if you can:
  » 'Sorry, I'd love to help, but I really don't have time right now …'
  » 'Sorry, but I must get this finished before I can do anything else …'
  » 'Have you asked Bob? He may be able to help …'
  » 'It's simple if you use XYZ software. Get Tech Support to show you how …'

76

✳ If they persist in the request, persist in the refusal and stick to your guns:
  » 'No, really, I do not have the time ...'
  » 'This job must take priority ...'
  » 'It may be only a ten minute job, but I don't have even five minutes to spare ...'

Keep calm
If you feel yourself getting angry at their inability to take 'no' for an answer, stop, count down from ten, calm down, and refuse again – with a smile.

How to say 'no' to the boss

This can be tricky, because:

✳ you shouldn't be refusing any reasonable request, and
✳ you may not want to admit that you can't cope with the job.

But if you don't say 'Stop!' now and then, your boss may keep piling on the work simply because he or she thinks that you are coping happily.

Before it gets too much, ask for a meeting. Keep calm, be reasonable, be helpful, but be realistic about the limitations of time and energy. The boss may have unrealistic ideas about how long things take to do. You may be overworking – giving jobs a higher level of detail and finish than they need.

What is expected of you?

You need to clarify expectations:

✳ How much work are you expected to do?
✳ How much time are jobs expected to take?
✳ If the task is over and above your normal workload, what other work is to be omitted or delayed to make way for it?
✳ Have your responsibilities increased since you first started?
✳ Has this been acknowledged?
✳ Is it still realistic?
✳ Are other people off-loading work on you unfairly?

How to say 'no' to friends and family

Unwanted invitations

First rule: start by thanking them for the offer.

Give a good reason for refusing, but only one. If you give more than one reason, they'll be taken as excuses.

If you want to, leave open the possibility of saying 'yes' another time.

> 'Thank you, but I've already got plans for that day …'
> 'Thank you, but I don't want to see that film …'

If they persist, repeat the refusal, perhaps using different words but with the same message:

> 'Sorry, no, I've already agreed to be elsewhere …'
> 'No thanks, I've read the review and I know I won't enjoy it …'

Excessive demands

Mutual help and co-operation is the essence of friendship and family life, but it's two way. If you feel that you are being put upon or asked to do more than your fair share of chores, use the same techniques as for saying 'no' at work.

It is important to try to make your stand before resentment damages relationships.

Co-operation is the essence of friendship and family life, but it's two way

81

● Are you carrying more than your fair share?

When to say 'yes'

You're scurrying around, struggling to get things done, time is running out, and someone says, 'Do you want a hand?'. What's stopping you from saying 'Yes'?

I don't say 'yes' because:

1 It will take longer to show them how to do it than to do it myself.
2 They won't do it as well as I will.
3 I don't want to owe them a favour.
4 I don't want people to think I need help.

Why are those bad reasons?

1 Possibly true this time, but next time, they will know how.

2 They will if you give them a chance to practise.

3 They are colleagues/friends/family – you are supposed to co-operate.

4 Everyone knows how much you achieve by yourself. You don't need to prove it all the time.

● How beautiful it is to do nothing, and then to rest afterward (Spanish proverb)

8 Limiting interruptions

You saw back in Chapter 3 how unnecessary breaks can increase the time it takes to get jobs done. Some of these breaks are directly under your control; others are caused by other people. All of them can be reduced or even eliminated:

* Filter your incoming phone calls.
* Control your outgoing phone calls.
* Create 'Not now!' times for uninterrupted work sessions.

Ins and outs
Limit your coffee/tea breaks to one mid-morning and one mid-afternoon. (This may also reduce your toilet breaks!)

Try not to break the flow on big jobs to deal with small jobs

Don't interrupt yourself

Try not to break the flow on big jobs to deal with small ones. Most emails, phone calls, filing chores (paper, electronic or fingernail), and the like can be done in an hour's time.

Make a list of little jobs. Deal with what you can one at a time when you have a convenient gap (see Chapter 4), and set aside time to deal with the rest.

Not Now!
This means you (and me)

Other people's interruptions of your work are relatively insignificant compared with the countless times you interrupt yourself.

Brendan Francis

Tame the phone (incoming)

There are two aspects to this: cutting down on unwanted calls, and making good use of the ones you do want.

Unwanted calls

* If you have a secretary or calls come to you through a switchboard, can they filter for you?
* If you have people who like to ring 'for a chat' during work hours, discourage them.
* Don't give your work phone number to anyone who doesn't need it.
* At home, sign up for the Telephone Preference Service to cut down on cold calling (http://www.tpsonline.org.uk)

When it's important that you are not interrupted, switch on the answering machine or turn off your mobile.

Phone efficiency

If a phone call does not result in an action of some sort, it was probably a waste of time. The action may simply be to get some information or a decision, and that could have been done during the call. If it's urgent and you can do it immediately, get it out of the way.

If further action is needed, log it:

* who called
* their contact number/email address/other details as needed

* what is to be done
* who is going to do it (if delegating)
* when it is to be done by.

Then act on it. Delegate the job, if necessary. Otherwise, allocate a time in your diary.

Tame the phone (outgoing)

Here are three ways to save time on your outgoing phone calls:

1 Filter out the unnecessary.
2 Don't interrupt other work to make calls.
3 Be properly prepared.

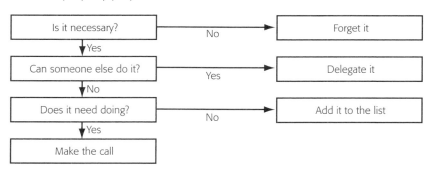

Is it necessary?	→ No →	Forget it
↓ Yes		
Can someone else do it?	→ Yes →	Delegate it
↓ No		
Does it need doing?	→ No →	Add it to the list
↓ Yes		
Make the call		

Phone time

1 Allocate one or two blocks of time each day for phone calls (and other little jobs).
2 At the start of a phone session, prioritize the list of calls.
3 Start with the most urgent/important, and work through – with proper preparation.

Preparation

You should prepare for a phone call as you would for a meeting:

* Why are you making the call? What action or information do you want to get from it?
* Are any papers or files relevant? Are they at hand? Do you need to read them?
* Are you ready to take notes?

Shut that door!

An office door gives you more control over your time. Let people know your rules:

* If it is open, you are available.
* If it is closed, you do not want to be interrupted.

You must stick to your rules.

* Leave it open except when necessary.
* Ignore any knocking when it's closed.

Virtual doors

But office doors are a luxury denied to most who work for larger organizations. If you don't have one, create your own virtual door. All you need is a 'Do not disturb' sign. However, you will get a better reaction from colleagues if you phrase it better, and if you also have a 'Welcome' sign when you don't mind being disturbed.

Write messages like these on either side of a piece of card (add colour if you can – red for 'Stop', green for 'Come in') and hang it or prop it where it will be visible to anyone approaching your workspace.

Not right now please

How can I help today?

No texts please ...

Text messaging needs to be kept firmly under control, but, used properly, it can save quite a bit of time.

The worst thing you can do is to read texts as they arrive. They are just the sort of little interruptions that can mess up a work session.

✳ Whenever you need to concentrate on the job at hand – and that should be most of the time – turn your phone off.

✳ If you need to keep the phone turned on, then at least switch off the new message notification.

... at least, not right now

If you have a short and simple question or answer, a text message is often the most time-efficient way of communicating it.

Compared with a phone call:

* You don't have to wait for them to answer.
* It doesn't matter if they aren't there or the phone is turned off.
* You don't get drawn into conversations that you don't have time for.

Read and send texts in any gaps (see Chapter 4), or deal with them along with other small jobs at the end of the morning and afternoon. (Why not at the start? See Chapter 10.)

9 Tweaking and twiddling

Computers make us more efficient and enable us to do more, faster. They can also be time wasters – and not just the obvious things such as playing Patience!

There are two key time sinks with office applications:

1 The formatting trap – too much time is spent making something look pretty, when it is the content that matters.
2 The search for exactitude – because numbers can be calculated quickly and accurately, the temptation is to keep trying to get the 'right' answer.

Computers can also be time wasters

There are many ways to waste time on a computer, and a lot of them look like work

It's the words, not the processing

Never mind the 'It ain't what you say, it's the way that you say it' approach: when it comes to written stuff, the words are more important than their presentation. What that means for time management is that you should not be spending more time making it look good than writing it.

There are four levels of formatting:

1 Zero – plain text – where the text is going to a professional for outputting.
2 Minimalist – using only bold and italic formatting and the alignment tools – for letters and memos.
3 Styled – using heading styles to create structure as well as formatting.
4 Template – giving you style and layout, for professional-looking brochures, leaflets and newsletters.

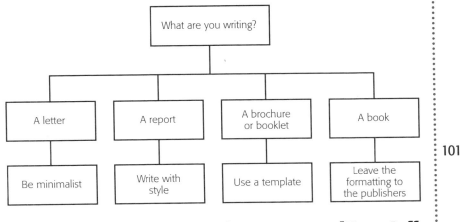

```
                    ┌─────────────────────────┐
                    │  What are you writing?  │
                    └─────────────────────────┘
                                 │
        ┌───────────────┬────────┴────────┬───────────────┐
        │               │                 │               │
┌───────────────┐┌───────────────┐┌───────────────┐┌───────────────┐
│   A letter    ││   A report    ││ A brochure    ││    A book     │
│               ││               ││ or booklet    ││               │
└───────────────┘└───────────────┘└───────────────┘└───────────────┘
        │               │                 │               │
┌───────────────┐┌───────────────┐┌───────────────┐┌───────────────┐
│ Be minimalist ││ Write with    ││ Use a template││ Leave the     │
│               ││ style         ││               ││ formatting to │
│               ││               ││               ││ the publishers│
└───────────────┘└───────────────┘└───────────────┘└───────────────┘
```

When it comes to written stuff, the words are more important than their presentation

Styles

In Word, a style is set of formats that are applied as one. The Heading 1 style, for example, will (normally – styles vary) change the font, add bold, set the colour,

Heading 1

Heading 2

Heading 3

make the text larger and put a space above and below it. Heading 2 will have a similar package, but with a smaller font and spaces.

Applying a style is quicker than changing each aspect of formatting separately, but also ensures that your headings are consistent, at their different levels, throughout the document.

Computers make it easier to do a lot of things, but most of the things they make it easier to do don't need to be done.

Andy Rooney

In versions of Word 2007 and above, the styles are ready to hand on the Home tab.

In earlier versions of Word, click Styles and Formatting on the Format menu to open the Styles sidebar.

Templates

If you want to produce a brochure, booklet, leaflet, invoice, or anything else with a complicated layout, then it is simplest to start from a template. This will have the layout, with prompts for what sort of text to put where, plus a set of styles. Picking a template takes minutes. Laying out and styling anything complicated takes ages.

To use a template as the basis of a document, start from New from the File (or the Microsoft Office Button) menu. Some templates will be present on your computer, and a wide selection is available online at Microsoft.

There is no charge for this online material, and no copyright restrictions, so take it and use it freely.

● A template will have the layout, with prompts for what sort of text to put where, plus a set of styles

Make your own templates

If you produce the same types of documents regularly, e.g. letters, create one with the fixed text (your address, etc.) in place, and the margins and styles set, then save using the 'Template' Save As option. Next time you want a letter, start your new document from this.

Spreadsheets: the limits of accuracy

One of the problems with spreadsheets is that they can calculate results to an incredible degree of accuracy. Why is that a problem? Because it can be misleading. If any of the figures in the spreadsheet are estimates, then any result produced using them cannot be accurate.

Anything involving future costs or profits will inevitably contain estimates, and the more estimates there are, the less reliable the final result will be.

'Estimate' is a fancy word for 'guess', and, although some people are better guessers than others, the only way to get an exact value for a future figure is to wait for it.

Nice round numbers

Estimates and any results calculated from estimates should always be expressed in nice round numbers, i.e. ending in '0' or '00' or '000'. This is to remind you and anyone else who uses the numbers that they are not accurate.

Where's the time-saving in all of this?

If you are ever working on budgets, sales projections, what-if scenarios or anything else that involves estimates, keep the limits of accuracy in mind and don't waste time trying to 'improve' the results.

10 Email overload and how to avoid it

There's a theory that 'infomania' – addiction to texting, email and the like – can lower our IQ. The constant stimulus of new messages raises the levels of noradrenaline and dopamine in the brain, reducing its capacity for complex thinking. Keep a record of your email usage:

* How often do you check for new messages?
* How many new message alerts do you get?
* How much time do you spend each session?
* How much time in total, each day?

Infomania can lower your IQ

If you can get your electronic communications under control, you won't just save time, you'll also keep your brain in better working condition.

Hacking through an email jungle is exhausting. Keep it under control and save yourself a lot of sweat

Mastering email messages

Email is a wonderfully simple, fast and economical communications system but it can take over large chunks of your life if you don't bring it under control. There are four prongs of attack:

* Limit the amount that gets sent to you.
* Restrict your emailing sessions.
* Deal with what arrives more efficiently.
* Keep tight control of old messages.

Spam

It should go without saying that you must have your spam filter turned on – either on the machine or at the email service provider, and set to at least the medium level of security.

Limiting access to the inbox

The email that is quickest to deal with is the one that isn't sent to you. To reduce the number of unwanted emails in your inbox:

✷ Limit who knows your email address – in particular don't put it on a website unless you have to.

✷ When delegating jobs, ask not to be copied in on emails unless there is a very specific reason.

✷ Unsubscribe from any mailing lists, unless you read them regularly.

The email that is quickest to deal with is the one that isn't sent to you

Session control

Unless there is a very specific reason why you must read new email messages as soon as they arrive, don't let them interrupt you.

In order of preference, to minimize interruptions:

1   Don't run your email software except during email time (see below).
2   Failing that, turn off the automatic check for new messages.
3   Failing that, turn off the alerts when new messages arrive.

Email time

Ideally, you should have only one or two sessions a day when you deal with email. These should be in allocated times at the start or end of the day, or of the morning and afternoon.

Zipping through the inbox

Get through emails quickly like this:

✱ Obviously spam: delete.
✱ Unknown sender, odd subject line: assume it's spam and delete.
✱ Copied or bcc'd to you: skim it, then file if it may be needed for
  reference, otherwise delete.
✱ To you: read it, reply if necessary and file or delete.

Filing email? Oh yes. The inbox is not the
only place to keep messages. Read on …

Organizing email

If you don't do something about it, your email inbox will clog up and slow you down. The more you have in there, the longer it will take you to find an old one if you need to refer to it again. (Full folders also slow down the email system, although they have to get very full before you'll notice it.)

Delete it

1 If you have no further need of an email message, delete it.

116

2 Empty the Deleted Items folder regularly – most systems have an option to empty it automatically at the end of a session.

3 Use the Compact Folders routine weekly. It tidies up message storage and speeds up the system.

Filing email

If you need to keep emails for future reference, then keep them where you can find them quickly.

1 Create folders for each project/client/type of work (or however you can sensibly group messages).
2 After you have dealt with a message, drag it from the inbox into its folder.
3 Drag copies of your messages from Sent to the appropriate folder.
4 When there are more than a few dozen messages in a folder, set up a new 'archive' folder within it and move the older ones to there.

If you don't do something about it, your email inbox will clog up and slow you down

Sending email

Cut down on your outgoing emails. You will save your own time, and the time of the people who would otherwise have to read them:

✴ Don't write them if you don't have to.
✴ Don't write any more than you need to.

Emails that aren't worth sending

✴ 'Got it, thank you!' Unless you've something more to say, acknowledge receipt only if there have been past problems with email or attachments, or if you need to for legal reasons.
✴ 'Copying to you for your interest ...' Unless you know that they really are interested.

Email is more reliable than snail mail. Do you write to people just to let them know you got their letter? And, likewise, do you expect people to acknowledge receipt?

KISS

Keep It Short and Simple – but do it properly. As with most things, time spent on preparation is time saved in the long run. If you are clear, you will avoid misunderstandings, which can waste a lot of time.

❋ Take a moment to think about what you need to write.

❋ Write it as briefly as possible.

❋ Run the spellcheck over it to pick up typos.

❋ Reread it to check that it says what it should.

Men won't read any email from a woman that's over 200 words long.

Doug Coupland